MW01341622

To..................................

From................................

Enjoy!! ☺

For Steve, for loving me and sharing
our life and
our gold daughters;
Caroline, Helen and Kate,
the inspiration behind this book.
"I <u>Love You Too</u>!"

A Green Kite Books
No part of this publication may be reproduced in whole or in part
without written permission from the publisher.
For information regarding permission, write to Green Kite Books
PO Box 2896, Southfield, Michigan 48037
greenkitebooks.com

ISBN 978-0-9824546-0-2

Printed in China

Love You Too

Sarah Sexton

Green
Kite

Books

"Love is so **<u>BIG</u>**

The more love you give
The more love you receive

And as you grow
So does your love
So does your heart
And so does the feeling
Of a compassionate being

Love travels to you, you, her and him
Love is the best
No competition
When you give love
Everyone wins

Love is not measured
Nothing that **BIG** has ever been
measured before
I guess if we tried you would start at the
floor

Your measuring would go and go and go
It would go past the walls shooting
straight out the door
Your love would be measured right past
planet Earth
Your _love tape_ would take you out
Into the great and grand and loving
universe

When you came back to land
You would understand
That your traveling did not have to take you out
Of the Milky Way
You only had to stay
At home
With your one-of-a-kind family
You would see...

Their hug is the only measuring to be done
Family's embrace whispers
'I love you today,
Much more than yesterday.
I cannot even imagine
My love for you tomorrow.'

Now when you walk out that door
Love does not always come easy
Yes, love is constant, complex,
And even cheesy

You will endure a time or two
Love's task stretched tall
Unclear, the most important lesson of all

The more love you give
The more love you receive

Never, never, never forget...
To <u>love you too</u>!

You are you!
A divine and special you
And on the busy, loving streets of special
you's
Put love and passion in your long list of
_To-do's_

You are teaching others
The message I taught you
And if you need a refresher
Come to my arms
For a **<u>BIG</u>** love hug

You are never too old
To grasp on
To hold
The love from others

The more love you give
The more love you receive

Now, take your kind thoughts
To create more peace
Teach with your lead
And always believe
To **<u>LOVE</u>**

And our world will truly succeed!"

About the Author:

Sarah Sexton, an American writer, is living abroad in England with her husband and three daughters. Sarah has an expansive resume loving other humans, animals and life. Sarah has an elementary teaching degree and a masters in reading. Her unique poetic message can be enjoyed by audiences of all ages. Sarah enjoys spending time with her family exposed to different backdrops the world provides. She is equally happy enjoying coffee in her pajamas at home.

Love You Too is Sarah Sexton's children's book debut.

About the Illustrator:

Sarah Sexton is also the illustrator for, Love You Too. Painting and drawing are passions for Sarah. Her heart pours onto the canvas and into her drawings. Look for a heart in each illustration of, Love You Too.

greenkitebooks.com

Logo Design by David L. Plante

Be your own author:

Can you tell somebody you love them today? What would you say? Write it down and tell them. Use colorful expressions. Use different colored pens to bring your writing to life. Write it as a story, poem or a list. Please let your imagination blast when expressing your love towards others!

Be your own illustrator:

Can you draw a picture of love? Draw your portrait, draw your family or draw your favorite animal. Mimic, Sarah and hide a heart or another significant symbol. Show a friend and have them find your hidden picture.